Giant Moth Perishes

Wave Books, Seattle and New York

Giant

Moth

Perishes

Geoffrey

Nutter

Published by Wave Books

www.wavepoetry.com

Wave Books titles are distributed to the trade by

Consortium Book Sales and Distribution

Phone: 800-283-3572 | SAN 631-760X

Library of Congress Cataloging-in-Publication Data

Names: Nutter, Geoffrey, 1968– author.

Title: Giant moth perishes / Geoffrey Nutter.

Description: First Edition. | Seattle : Wave Books, [2021]

Identifiers: LCCN 2020038259 | ISBN 9781950268207 (hardcover)

ISBN 9781950268191 (paperback)

Subjects: LCGFT: Poetry.

Classification: LCC PS3614.U88 G53 2021 | DDC 811/.6—dc23

LC record available at https://lccn.loc.gov/2020038259

Designed by Crisis

Printed in the United States of America

9 8 7 6 5 4 3 2 1

First Edition

Wave Books 093

for Kerry Vann

The Faerie Queene   1

Pyrotechnicians   3

Summer Trip to Iceland   5

The Opera Called *Boys Against Girls*   7

The City of Underachievers   9

The Octagon House   11

The Wind Farms   13

Invocation   15

That Was the Summer   16

Mysterious Travelers   18

Juan Fernández Firecrown   21

The Constitution   23

A Yellow Vase in Its Environs   24

The Lost Continent   25

Clocks That Strike Only at Sunset   27

The Actuarial Fallacy   30

Silent G   32

The Houseplant That Suffered from Daydreaming   33

A Complicated Clock   35

Fireworks   37

Let Us Look at One of Those Teardrops   39

The Figurehead   42

Tata Conglomerate   44

What Does This Phrase Mean to You?   46

A Story about Helicopters   48

The Land of Mighty Insects   51

Anthropomorphic Landscape   52

9 What?   55

Study of Blue   57

When I Was in Your Presence   58

Noh   59

The Curiously Parallel Inclination of a Girl's Head   60

The Sea and Its Children   61

Refinery in a Winter Landscape   63

The Orphan Girl in the Wood Named Ericka Scissors   65

The Sea That Has Become Known   67

Family Seated around a Table   69

The City That Would Never Be Finished   70

An 18th-Century Sunset with Samuel Delany   72

A Voice Recording   74

What Happens to the World When You Close a Book?   76

Reading Gibbon   78

Glass in the Heyday of Cutting   79

Deneb in Zenith   81

Giant Moth Perishes   83

The Gathering Sea   84

Again, somehow, one saw life, a pure bead.   —Virginia Woolf

Giant Moth

Perishes

The Faerie Queene

I sleep while reading, and sleep
while writing a poem, and I sleep
while I'm talking or walking toward
the concrete spires and pylons
of the fish hatchery or Nimbus Dam—
so why can't I sleep while sleeping? Why
must I count how many houses have
a locust in them or scan the columns
of the *Textile Manufacturer's Monthly*
for the price of bolts of silk from Shāndōng Shěng?
I was reading *The Faerie Queene* for hours:
and the changeling of a virgin conjured from snow
became the cold protagonist
while her flesh-and-blood twin, a real girl,
stepped into an open boat, pushed from shore
and floated toward the sea, perhaps towing
the honored form of the great red fish
behind the flotilla. On the riverside
the hordes flow silently over the land:
the army ants and the carpenter ants.
What relevance to me and the rain that I half listened to,
the 21st-century rain? Perhaps

you can point the way toward the seawall
of our childhood, where the only governing force
is the fresh gale blowing in over waves
to dwell in vine-draped caves in cliffsides;
and all things of August appear
then disappear in turn, only
to become September.

(The child opens—then closes—the textbook:
the ornate veil of remembrance is lifted
revealing a row of saplings, each a yearling
filled with green sap: *In the North they tell*
of a fish three thousand miles long.
It leaps from the water, and between its leap
and the splash as it falls back into the sea,
you will have grown into adulthood.)
Life, according to the *Dictionary*
of the Underworld, is called "the book";
but it is also called "from now on."

Pyrotechnicians

Came the Pyrotechnicians.
When the suspension bridge over Niagara
was to be erected, came the kite⁄fliers
to draw the cable over to the far shore,
came the Pyrotechnicians to show
how the kite string, though weak, nonetheless
draws toward Heaven, holds its possessor
fast anchored within the veil, and the bridge
holds its possessor close to the far shore.
And came the Pyrotechnicians to show
illumination, stratagem, blue bergamot,
and Theodore Roosevelt was present, too,
there at that day's centenary. Does he have
the power not to create the un⁄liftable stone
that he bears aloft, the eight⁄angled triangle
unimagined by Euclid—he can, and does.
Yet in the midst of his restraint came barium
for green; came copper for blue; came aluminum,
finally, for silver and strontium salts for red, like Thespians
mirroring the Sun King, or Oberon, bright phosphorus
aflame on Mercury. Came the Pyrotechnicians

in town-planning councils in Lansing or Aurora,
stringing dragon kites across the sky,
circular, incessant, calm with linearity, cyclopean—
their dew is on the meadowsweet, green-gold.

Summer Trip to Iceland

FOR CHRIS JONES

And on our summer trip to Iceland
they served us yellow strawberries
as I rose from sleep in the stucco house;
so here you are beside the oval sea—
and like the sea, you have been
an urban planner, weather observer,
wonder counselor: a new kind of person
washed ashore from the depths of the sea.
And here the aurora can be your child
that walked with you beside the sea
among the cool refractions,
while you were planning an alternate city
built on segments and warmth reaching in through summer,
and the toll of bells at intervals signaling growth,
for time and growth are games played by children.

Rose-tinted lamps shine blue in the snow
in front of an oblong teahouse
where sharp adjacencies grew rounded
and blunt with the deepening hour.
This was the place I'd imagined,

in the common room of a seaside resort
as a guest there, and grew ill and weak
with the deepening hour
and reached for a marbled book on the high shelf,
a book about lands cold and vast as Neptune.

For each thing constructed also grows—
and after a time, you were free in the trailing vines
while the blueing egg shined, and the seashells,
the marble or the zephyr cone,
whispered while you walked among them,
and the geothermal steam of Nesjavellir,
and the green turf-covered houses
like the deep tolling of the chapel bells
and desolate green twilight on the snow
where you walked, able planner,
all formed a shifting image of a country you called home
where you are reading a book with one page—
a book that takes a lifetime to read.

The Opera Called *Boys Against Girls*

Yet all that summer it was boys against girls
when the giant girls and boys were fighting,
where past was prologue, and all bore down
on one another in the radiance of flooded land
where the mezzo-soprano sang the dizzy aria.
Did the gender binary ripen with you inside it,
curled like a lima bean, surrounded by giants?

This was the school where we learned the sweet science.
We had opened the door into summer, and passed back through
into winter where the taskmistress greets us. We were once
common men, we were all common men, but now
we are common no longer. I was a student there too,
pupil and pugilist, on Rush Street, the Mecca of clip joints,
along strip malls, and sunrise, and strip joints.

This was the fanfare. This was the fanfare
for the common man. For the common man
grew unruly in the dark arena, cauliflowers growing
in place of each ear, crumpled yams in place
of the lips, the face a tuberose, the head a mandrake,
until you were left to sleep beneath the bamboo

and octagonal windows, a dwarf in the fistic
landscape. And the common woman grew
into a womanhood towering over the earth,
where the great bell was tolling. It said,
"You may see yourself as a wolf or a bear
or some other kind of changeling flummoxed
in a cold blur brought on by changes. And are you
a Trojan, Attic, tasked with living
in the flesh's bulk whose demands are unforgiving?"
This was the year of our misgivings.

The City of Underachievers

Far North,
in the landlocked town of Norilsk, trucks
are taking loads of nickel from the mine
to the refinery on unthawed roads at dawn—
but in the morning sky some lights can still be seen:
Red Mars, the Marvelous; Blue Venus, Visionary,
Vainglorious; Pale Neptune, Cold as Nepenthe;
Storm-Bedizened Saturn, Taciturn, its disks
of amethyst and jasper, Saturnine.

Far from the arctic city of Norilsk
in the permafrost zone: The angry
green-yellow apple kvetches; the lovelorn
apricot turns to the sun and then away;
the overwrought walnut feels accosted,
falls to the black earth and pretends to sleep;
rain scatters on the obtuse tulip bulbs.
But the holly is cynical and touchy.
There, that lone acanthus is first among
the mediocrities: a dullard.
The showy lily is tragic, and slatternly.
The heliotrope thinks he is special,

a philosopher or an astronaut.
The celandine is small. The anemone
is in his own world, and all day dreams
about the sea. Look at the Brazil nut—
brooding, sick of soul. The quince
is just neurotic. The violet is frigid.
But the thistle feels exalted—

Far from the arctic city of Norilsk
the birds of April: some in the crooked tree
by the firehouse; some in the orchard;
others scattered in the sky above the silos,
others in barns or under bridges.
Are the birds sad? When asked
they might respond, "We are rather
ambivalent, truth be told." But they
have little else to say.
Will the earth repudiate its sad
and diffident children?

The Octagon House

On our visit we stayed at the octagon house—
and were sleepless in view of the eight-sided land.
Uncombed grass webbed the sides of the angled veranda.
And on one side of the eight-sided land
the incandescent lanterns of the doll shops flickered on.

And we stretched out to sleep in the blue rosemaling
houses of Uvdal, and the melon-colored houses
of Forget-Me-Not, under the cool, peninsular hills
beyond the spruces and glass-covered A-frames.

And we were stressed out and wakeful on Zoloft
and Asendin in the atomic houses of Pripyat,
and insomniac in the blue-stanchioned shadows
of Shasta Dam—and through the blackberry vines
that covered the round cement window
grew dizzy watching distant water
falling silently over the spillway.
Some heaven-shining-august child
seemed to be petting a deer
that was grazing yellow grass
beyond the hydroelectric building.

And we were somnambulists at sunset in Anchorage
where German tourists had gathered around
a gargantuan piece of jade, saying nothing,
while it revolved there before them, cold
as a fire clock steeped in withering rebukes.

And we dozed in the bean-pod houses in the fields
under the mushroom umbrellas of Poisonville.
Our nerves were stretched out on the grass
like sea kelp or sea nerves that have washed up
and been strung out to dry in the high seagrass.
And we came to a boil in the teakettle houses,
became bird people living off the grid, became
rebels, bearcats, masters of inadvertency.

Will you then lie spent on the cool
mushroom bed when you are down again
by the mill-track and the fernery?
Will you contemplate the stupid grapefruit,
the tedious eggplant, the intellectual thorn?
And will you wake up fresh and confused
in a place you have been borne to for asylum
like a chick just hatched from a fire-colored egg?
And will you see the starships
drifting over rain-colored mountains?
The copper-streaked leaves
that shine in the pattering rain?

The Wind Farms

Sunset: making and mending.
Floating cities. Machines
for bleaching and dyeing.
Sailing past the volcano; the strength
of the weak; the finger of the past
pointing toward us—then the entire
hand opening out in a gesture
of greeting; clouds aflame above
the Houses of Monstrosities and
the Houses of Peace, both
on equal terms. Garden cities;
strip malls and garbage dumps;
observations of the wind flow
over natural terrains; shelter
defined by the decreasing wind speed
caused by an obstacle standing
on a hillside; the height
and length of the obstacle;
the three blades turning clockwise
lazily. Black mold spreading
through a crust of bread.
The slow-growing, long-lived,
sun-loving lichens in the cool
mountains. The plash of oars

in a lake the color of sunlight.
Five curious eggs on the shelf
of the wonder cabinet; a sundial;
machines, starlight, fire, lightning;
great coral reefs in decline, birds
firing off cannons, hares
beating drums; three men running
without hats across a field
toward a burning airship;
the harrowing; the planting,
the harvest; the gathering-in
and the bringing harvest home.
The great lens of the observatory
turning toward one section of the sky
to regard the Swan and the Clock,
the Furnace and the Holder of the Snake,
the Carpenter's Level and the Lyre.
A great fiberglass sphere filled
with sparrows. The sea and the rain;
the rising sea level eating away
the retaining wall; cylindrical
rooms for the children; the glorious
uncertainty of the Law.

Invocation

Mountains, valleys, deserts,
flowers, trees, and children,
listen: today is the first day
of spring. A big ball of shadow
is sitting on the grass. And this
ball is casting another shadow,
a bigger and more shadowy
shadow. Gather round us, hills,
lakes, rivers, and children,
and all strange new landforms,
make way for the grapes
and their timely arrival,
do not obstruct them with
your selfish plans for summer,
your fears of winter. A vast
countryside with towers round
and square, O come you birds
and green insects, fruit trees
and brooks, the world is weaving
its dark ball of newness.

That Was the Summer

That was the summer that the stranger,
the mandarin, settled in the park
on the far side of the pond. (It is hiding.)
They have all gone (the people),
they have crossed a border pool
or larger body of water. You loved
the month of July, where the honeybee's
quiescence came as one of many troubles
thundering down upon us;
you were rowing a small boat
on the pond with a girl of the Sunshine
family name (derived from a word that means
Sunshine)—bird people living
off the grid, Mennonites and Seminoles
disguised as woodlarks. And you
are the month of July, retracting
its sting, seeing nothing until you are
invisible, an idea, but one that is walking
in a line through grass, sometimes a boy,
sometimes a girl in your majority.
Wrap the blue sheets inscribed with Japanese

epistolary love poems around the branch
of walnut with those pear-stems, or with phlox:
and then be nothing but a child
swimming in the center of a diamond.

Mysterious Travelers

I ran into someone on the street.
Someone I—or was it you—
went to preschool with? The building
was a brick thumb, and we,
or you, were housed there, in a room
with a round transom above
a cabbage-colored door. We ate
cabbage there, crab cabbage.
I was always the last one done—
to your embarrassment—which meant
we had to scour pans and nutmeg
grinders, while all the rest repaired
to the ilex and the baseball diamond.
A thumb, they say, is small,
but it also is opposable—"for humans,"
we two small young humans, members
of a small revanchist opposition.
There was a farmhouse, you know,
with a blond alpaca. We punned
on her name. The wattage
was low in the fluorescent bulb,
and in the course of day you opened yourself

to discipline and remorse,
perched on the stub of a green
goblin-like knoll of petrified stone.
There were petrified tears there,
marbled olive-green, lacquered with
the varnishes made for japanning tin.
In class we learned about topology
and dawn in Nova Zembla, and how
to identify birds in starlight,
how to speed-read, and were taught
to be constantly on alert
without a moment's pause,
to turn ours into a mushroom country
by cultivating mushrooms scientifically.
And in the thick book under the ferns,
clouds of locusts, termites and white ants,
the giant snake with poison eyes
emerged from the depths of the sea.
We shortened ropes by wetting them,
undid saffron knots for rough brocade,
and memorized *The Sceptical Chymist*.
As a bell tower is round, the beldam's hair
was covered with Oriental beetles.
We set the parameters, then forget them,
read through the ideologue

for the gummed adherents
that we might recite them haltingly,
pupils half reciting "Kubla Khan."
Was it Keats who said
Come to me faster than light,
where philosophers gowned in red-gold invite
all Anti-Deathists to join them?
How do the words dream together?
How to make you live inside their dream?

Juan Fernández Firecrown

The fuse that would destroy mankind
was lit and burning—but it was burning
slowly, and would continue burning forever
as he slept, deep-frozen, in the interval of thaw
between season and season, the April
month between child and man, gray-green
sleep that dreams of the fullness of time.
And after waking, he wandered between open groves
in his lilac helmet with the diamond thumbprint, and toward
and among all Strange Antagonists, Odd Pincover
and Mr. Hatmaker, the Panjandrum
and the child in the Parable of the Vat of Black Dye.
And watch how he constructs his nest
from materials readily available: wood ash, decaying
fruit, fluorspar and a sheet of pale green foolscap.
But that afternoon his plans were disrupted
by a message reading: "To the Fearless One,
the Formless One—You are directed to appear
at my palace tomorrow." On the waves
of the Sea of the Blossoming of April,
where our virginity is not lost (we are transforming

out of it and back again) and time will not obtain,
the Sea King brooks no opposition. He leaves
the original and glorious pill
like a single teardrop in your hand
in which your reflection is shattered.

The Constitution

In the revised and updated edition
of the United States Constitution,
nostalgists and dreamers were dreaming.
And one had unshelved a volume in the lobby
of the hotel by the urban sea: "To not touch
again the center of all things, where anthracite
glitters at the core, black like moonlight . . ."
Those were the words that opened a long chapter
somewhere in the middle of that book.
There are closet dramas, *Lotus-Eaters Awake*
one among them, that teach our grim inheritance,
that to be monsters, floating creatures,
stung by jellyfish or jellyfish themselves
among sleek dolphins mindful of their homelessness,
always barely on the verge. And yet
it wants to protect us from ourselves,
who might barely deserve protecting.

A Yellow Vase in Its Environs

We live in our own experience,
like this yellow vase, standing
in its cool green environs,
almost reptilian as the sea;
and the sea was a blue vase broken,
then put back together piece by piece
and set beside the sea. No use is too
alien for the ceramic birds of April
and the painted branches warming in the sun.
None too relevant to your own life as you
see it, tapering toward an entrance gate
of wakeful living. And if, on the tabletop
beside the vase, an apple core goes brown
amid some bent cigarette butts in a shell
of abalone put there as an ashtray,
its iridescence smudged and blackened,
and the gears of trucks are grinding
on Avenue Melodica as they head into the sky—
these "mere things" are World Things, yet
private as a sea dialogue. O what name
or title suits your greatness,
Aldiborontiphoscophornio?

The Lost Continent

Strange shapes carved on the sea cliffs—
yes, strange . . . strange . . . but how?
Show, don't tell! Immense
stone monuments stood upright
on the patches of red coral—on what
sorts of ships were they conveyed here?
And those strange petroglyphs
carved on the sea cliffs
seem to want to tell us something
concerning a subject like time or the sea,
an ultramarine chronology, suburban
passages that smolder far below
the city near the earth's core;
or their far future, just as cryptic
in their burying and unburying—
Show the cities! The derricks
gently lifting an invention
and its thousand simulacra from the deck
of the Hanjin freighter docked
along the pier of the harbor port—
the brine-streaked bulbs of kelp,
the decorative lotus blossoms

edged around the borders of our mother earth
behind which rise the giants,
monuments for lightships
laving the edges of the sky. Show
don't tell!

Clocks That Strike Only At Sunset

And if we go down into the cool
spaces under the cliffs where the sea
fills the tide pools at sunset, the grotto
like a great door that opens out onto a garden
where a giant turnip and its fleshly roots
are drinking cool water spilling from the basin
of a fountain and its snarl of ornaments and dolphins;
and if symbols carved in the Rosetta stone
can list the rules of transactions involving vineyards
or abolishing taxes, or the granting of amnesty
by Ibis-headed Thoth—compared to which simple rain
is more thrilling, even when seen
falling on the canal beside the scrapyards—
and if the damselfly, amiable and half-transparent,
goes off into the yellow sky to rear her children;
and if you haven't seen her; and if
you're blown out to sea only to be listed
in the Registry of Lost Things, one among
others—the jeweled comb; a bit of vitreous
china and a wedding ring; the half-transparent
child of the damselfly—and if you fell asleep
in the solarium, where near movable screens

made to look like real flowers the gardener
is using wire to tie the blue body
of the damselfly to a blade of grass
to make it look alive; and if you are there
among the hothouse orchids and the ferns
in your red velvet smoking jacket as you snip
some roses with grape scissors, thinking
the cynical thoughts of a man
who has found his place in the world,
a place of relative seclusion in a house
full of clocks in the form of chariots;
of clocks in the form of eggs; of eggs;
of clocks in the shape of houses;
in the shape of crickets, clocks in the form
of cats, of cubes of ice, of cubed cats;
clocks with asps inside, with eggs
that open by unscrewing; with mirrored
clocks and clocks that strike only at sunset
or clocks painted with a prospect of blue
Luna City as seen from green hills: then lay blame
for this and any other thing you might regret
at the feet of the cat, who nonetheless
is innocent—who looks at you with gentle
acceptance, as if to say, "I know who,
and even more, *what* you are—and I accept all,

forgive all; you can pretend, and I can
pretend along with you; and like the Parable
of the Grass Veils, that parted so the lions
were visible sunning themselves or sleeping
near the trees, I will be one among them,
and you will feel glad to be among the living."

The Actuarial Fallacy

I promised myself I wouldn't say
what I expected to say, nor even
something else: but what else?
And while we fill in a few hours
till sunset, we might ask: why
do we write poems? Hysterics?
Wonderment? Amnesia?
The reassignment of a misfit
identity to something better,
green mind for Saint John of Neptune?
I've been wondering, though
you need not answer. If to measure
time, a thing archaic: a cord
and colored threads tied with knots
that might record accounts
or thread a statutory grass greener
than the Pandects of Justinian; one
knot might stand for a volcano—
though looking nothing like it!
Or the quills of a porcupine
might be oracular, or an artificial
intelligence in wavering copper,

sharp to the touch. And Legend,
like growth of the soil, moves
too slowly to see, unplanned,
taking soundings where a vast
transitivity prepares for the future.
I invite you to just sit down now
(if you have no pressing obligations)
in the shadow of 666 Fifth Avenue,
and as in a dream where futurity
works itself out in fits and small flames—
look at the fluttering leaves
before you, they are simple gifts,
walled off in thoughtless, unnerving joy—
and though they are filled with a gentle sense
of concern and acceptance . . . aren't they?
they don't seem to care about you at all—

Silent G

"Design" is a word with a silent
G—so is "sign" and "reign."
And "laugh" . . . that too? "Migraine" has
a G that's too loud: it's rough,
like grit, and gilt⁄edged, and thus
bright—too bright to look at straight⁄on
with a headache, though benign.
You can spell "þe" with the sovereign thorn,
Beowulfian or, if you'd prefer, Icelandic,
though it looks like "be," open, admiring
& yellow as the pink⁄edged sulphur's wing.
Would Xerxes be there too, with triple X
to whip the Hellespont, or sail upon
the pterodactyl's archaeopteryx—so be it.
As you can see, the silent letters
make a noise, or noises—but steeped in blue
tea, what of invisible Z that sounds out
among the populace distributed around
the Cities of the Page? Come, we must
be lapidary, as in an iceboat in the sun.
Then we might find those chthonic
words that make no sound.

The Houseplant That

Suffered from Daydreaming

Like electricity,
as simple in practice
as it is confusing in theory,
our feelings move through us, as in a corridor
sealed from the pressures of the reservoir.
And you can switch on a bank of lights
and the green tile walls are bathed in fluorescence
as far as the eye can see.

Against the long life of the slow-growing
planet, still they grow more slowly.

Did we grow up to be free-lovers (so-called)
as if Icelandic among Oneida Perfectionists
in the thoroughgoing American sunshine,
Mr. Zeal-of-the-Land? Where all
might grow angry, red-tipped grass
among candle-storms, then fall away?
Likely . . .
And the wind comes down from the headlands

open to the sunset like jeweled boxes
or a case for needles, painted with cranes
in water reeds; the tranquillity of gardens,
and the fury of the fighter.

And we are strong like the ancient Greeks,
fighters among grapes
who send themselves fighting
toward awareness
of their origin, or apple girls
in the first flush of youth
who have yet to join the "human pageant."
Then they are washed
in the green blood of the lamb
and become mere people
like the rest of us.

And the moon's "systems of bright streaks"
as the observers of stars have been calling them
for centuries are far away,
yet they too force a sea change,
as the north wind alters the behavior
of refractory children.

A Complicated Clock

Here, let's look at a complicated clock.
Hear its winding, vibrant as a séance,
and as cryptic—a rarity. It seems
the humble clockmaker wished to address
the problem of time—to tell by showing.
Showing what? The ticktock trove of unguents
made from lavender, and the crushed thicket,
the scent of rain in Philadelphia,
the wisteria cold in Utrecht. Look:
here is a thing to polish time by: a spell,
a fractal of anaphora:
a night in Labrador, the maladroit
swim beneath the fireworks near the canal.
Their beryl light streaks the shy marigold.
Earth bends her waterfalls and lakes, burning
with topology, and it might dizzy or derange
her children; but she is merciful and strange
and grants us a stillness in her turning.
Friend, in People's Revolution, behold
the people's enemy, poised at Café Royale
in useless pursuits: games of chess, or quoits
with thrush or ne'er-do-wells in the agora

beneath the bronze statue of Mademoiselle
ten Boom, perusing the plates in a book
about orchids in Orchidelphia;
or learning to play a giant cricket
like a polished zither—nothing urgent:
the wheat stands tall, and all is growing.
So without regret or shame I confess
that this poem makes no discovery, redeems
no fault—it ends as it began: in blue faience,
the hiss of rain; the gold and bending stalk.

Fireworks

Time Rain. Waterfall.
Catherine Wheel spins for the
Czarina. Ring pledges troth.

Chrysanthemum cultivated
for fire. Flying Diamond
cut by the lapidary, winged.
Strobe and Bengal Fire
for the polity.

Triangular Chrysanthemum,
prismatic
Summer Storm.

Jumbo Saturn. Flying Gem.
Color Bomb and Roman Candle.
Fly, Aeroplanist, fly to Sea World.
Spinning Flash. Mahatma,
spin blue flax for fustian.

Peony, Friend Ship sails, Lotus blossoms
near constellation Swan, a Spinning Flash.
A Cherry Flash. Confucius.

Reckoning Barrage.

Great sentinel fires
seen from space. Flying wheel.
Tricolor Fountain placed upright
on soft earth and ignited.

Biplane and Dragonfly;
Sparrow and Lacrosse;
Stone-of-Red and Gentle-Mighty;

the fiery Tamerlane
of Happiness has its incessant
day in the sun.

Orioles
sing for its return.

Let Us Look at One

of Those Teardrops

In a typical postwar American town in 1957,
in a ranch-style house on Aluminum or Oak Street
on the wood-paneled wall of a bedroom, above
the bedside table where a cigarette smolders
in a crystal ashtray embossed with the logo
of Zim's in orange lettering, there hangs
a painting of a girl with huge round eyes.
She is a child of perhaps twelve.
Her hair is straw-yellow, like corn to stuff
a corn-husk doll. Judging by her dress
she has spent the night in an ash heap.
She is holding a terrified-looking cat.
She is standing in front of a blank wall
of a building streaked with earth tones.
And a single teardrop flows from each
enormous eye, each teardrop big and glinting.
Let us look at one of those teardrops.

One day sailing, one executive,
on the deck of his small boat one summer,

drinking his bottle of beer on open sea,
was caught in a glittering mist blown in from the sea.
It was some kind of magical mist from the sea
that makes fathers vanish forever. It might
have made him shrink like Gulliver
to the size and texture of a spice,
or a pink or emerald grain of sand, or turned
him into a fish, or simply made him vanish.
And so this executive was overcome by that mist
and lost and gone forever . . . goodbye . . . goodbye . . .

On shore a boy and girl were eating lunch
out of an erstwhile violin case: papaya
and oysters, agave and sea kelp for salt and sweetener.
They have eloped together having only just met;
and now, among the waving grass and the sisterly
things that also follow no logic, preceded
here in expectancy by sunlight on the ice plant,
they break their long fast: "How many cats
grew up in your hometown? Who paid
to feed them? Was the city green as a tree stump
or blue as an atom summer nights?" "Was Mélisande's
convolvulus scattered in sunbeams?" "How tall
is God?" The girl lived
in a phosphorescent dome with cement bay windows,

strips of greenish paint curling in the salt air.
Tall eucalyptus trees brushed the sky.
The boy was abashed, having until late been killing time
from age to age, cloud-sculptor, glimmer
of starlight rising with the rays of Somerset,
one among people by the lakes of the sea
and living on a ball of wire
where the glassy vertical ships are set on end
along the sky for lightning-catching towers.
The sky behind them is brownish, gray,
then gray-violet, shading to lavender, blue-gray,
pearl-gray shading to deep purple, blue-gray.
Now let us say goodbye to them. Goodbye . . . goodbye . . .
And our true penitent tears turn to solid pearl . . .

The Figurehead

And the figurehead was standing tall
its shoulders bare in the cool rain
its feet in the heather's omnipotent dew.
The elements are doing their steady work,
carving away at its features, turning
the delicate scrollwork into rounded bulges
and smoothnesses. One day, maybe long
in the future, zealots and patriots
will tether its appendages to mules
or bulky workhorses and pull it down—
pull it right down into the sea.
Strange flags will fly from the buildings
in the cold air blowing in from the Sea
of Afflictions where "the rose is not so sweet
on the tree as it is on the sill."
But until then, the swallows
cleave their way through the pathless air
to build their nests in hidden grooves, from hair,
bunting, bits of electric wire,
in eaves and mullions, bell turrets, wall-hooks
and decorative rails. Through the dark
and viscous sea the fish steer their course

back to the river where they were spawned.
Satellites are being sent into space—
they are like dewdrops snatched away by the sun.
The sun rising through hawthorn:
it was an affirmation of some sort.
While a man is stringing the harp,
he sounds a string here and there, not for music,
but for construction: when it is finished
it shall be played for melodies—. Let us see
how far his work has progressed,
as the human heart is fashioned for future
joy: the figurehead.

Tata Conglomerate

Opalescent globes of pure force appear
in various places around the world.
Take Tata. Would one call Tata
a pellucid ball of sexual energy? Would your Tia
Rosette in Guayaquil consent
to Tata Salt or tune into Betty La Fea
with the satellites of Tata Sky?
Eight O'Clock Coffee is Tata.
Tata Optical. Tata BlueScope Steel. Tata
Bearings. Tata Africa. The IT guys
from Maharashtra all
had worked for Tata (at one time or another)
in Mumbai or other places—and to Tata
might one day return. (One project
manager—Amandeep—had seen
a real beheading in Dubai [there
for resource training (under auspices
of Tata)].) Tata Steel. Tata Motors. Tata
Power. It's all Tata. They're all talking about Tata.
One Tata representative came to SonicNet
while we were running algorithms,
with the book by the op-ed columnist

contending that the earth was flat
from Singapore to Seoul to Cupertino,
this to quietly militate for Tata
(for all the tech guys, even coders,
are quietly being x'ed out by redundancy—
their roles outsourced to Tata).
Tata Ceramics. Tata Gutta-Percha.
You can sip Tata Agni Tea,
named for the Vedic god of fire, Agni,
as one missile too was named,
blasting over sea spray singing;
or Golden Milk with turmeric
and saffron, cardamom, and ghee.
We love Tata. The Tata Soda Ash
Extraction Plant in Tanzania.
The Terror Gang or Speed Trap
Racket. Villagers protesting
construction of a wall for Tata's steel
plant through their ancient village, shot
by soldiers at Kalinganagar, Odisha.

What Does This Phrase Mean to You?

But what does this phrase mean to you:
"People in glass houses should not throw stones."
Does it mean you might break things, these things
or others not yet named, nor dreamed of?
Or that the wasps outside in the bundled grasses
are visible, extravagant and copper, and electric
tempests flash? Some people collect small glass shoes,
of green frosted glass, milk blue or Nile green;
or persimmon-colored baby-shoe toothpick holders;
or slightly iridescent boot-shaped cologne bottles.
Others prefer a petrified seahorse; still others
a Japanese sunfish lantern, or teapots
shaped like cats, or aeronautics. Maybe
you count yourself one among them. Or maybe
you're an oversized man, stomping around
in big shoes, in jungle boots or waffle-stompers,
a bull in a china shop knocking things off shelves.
It all comes back around to what seems real,
the fruit that appears in Aesop's fable then disappears
again into a watery idea, its relevance transparent,
its surface easily shattered, an apple made of glass.
It's a familiar saying, an adage, and means just what it says.

And just as long as you're its creature, and its subject,
will you just sleep in that big armchair in the sunlight,
like a cat the color of cinnamon, the sun streaming
through the windows, a cat in an enormous chair,
the embers of the sunset all around you?

A Story about Helicopters

The people in the houses along the shore
were complaining about the helicopters—
in the houses shining as a honeydew, fronts
with light-blue stenciling intricate as watch parts—
they were militating frequently and passionately
with a brilliance unequaled, all in the name
of hatred for the helicopters and the rumbling
of their chopping.

In the colder zones of the symposium,
the people organized and militated, agitated,
reached the high-water mark, and signed
the papers scented with oil of anise and verbena.

Oh why did they hate the helicopters? They
are diamond seeds on the hyacinths
blooming giant in the sunset. They are zinc
fish with wings. Do you hate them, too?
The mirror of the heart reflects our waking dreams,
and the dreams that haven't yet wakened you.

But then one day the papers came back
with a kind of blush of victory, signed
by the inspector of machinery, his seal
a weeping willow in silver
set in Johnson Wax.
And along with the papers
a book the size of an airmail stamp called
Rules on the Regulation of Railway Travel
on Sundays and the Pattern of Winds at Sea.
Was that what they had been waiting for?
And the meetings in the agora
were once and for all dispersed—and a cheer went up
for the aristocracy of clocks, a song
of submarines and bismuth.

Now was the time for the growth of the soil.
They were bringing in summer for everyone.
And bamboo was growing in the vacant lot,
growing to the sun, and hotels were shining
in the orchard and the town.
They loved their houses set on the tip
of a cliff and leaning down across the viaducts.
And the Rainbow Monitor saw to it that sperm
lay green and lucent on the mons veneris.

The gifted people were ordained for life
at the Life Science Church on Cardinal Street
and took turns scaling the fuzzy zenith.
And the helicopters, like Pure Minds high up,
were blobs of blue geranium on cloth,
and merged upon a principle, gently,
until it was annihilated.

Well—you wanted to hear a story, and I
wanted to tell one. Now it's time to go
to sleep—God bless you child,
I see you're already dreaming.

The Land of Mighty Insects

The cat remembers the secret you shared
with her on a night that seems to have passed
a century or a century and a half ago.
Long past midnight, insomniac, and the private
and celebratory pod reserved for your party
at neon-green Koreatown. This
was a cobalt cat curled on an overstuffed chair
overspread with a fringed gold counterpane.
Time passes. And one day, when you strike up
a park bench acquaintance with some stranger,
and the city is glittering behind him,
glittering and splintering with glass and flares,
the idea just on the tongue was the same secret,
and you long for a lover to go with the secret.
The stranger stands tall as an ultimatum.
And you are as one who has spent her entire life
living high in the branches of a tree, surviving
off its fruit while giant insects rage below.

Anthropomorphic Landscape

One day, in order to have a more perfect
union, they will rebuild the United States
on the surface of the moon. Its buildings
and its farms, its lakes and canyons,
its offices, the dendriform columns
of the Johnson Wax Administration Building
and the Cigarette Growers League—
all its great destinations, natural
and man-made, and the entire populace
will be scattered among the lunar craters,
the landforms and the water features, and close
beside the ancient sea called the Sea That Has Become
Known or the Lake of Summer or the mountain
range called Albrecht Penck. Or further
and more glorious, the Great Red Spot
on Jupiter, its methane storms crackling
above the Great Plains. Tractors
and combines work amid pink grains
of salt the size of houses. Or it could be
on Everest, for instance (the highest place
on Earth where, surely, it can do no harm).

Or even the deepest under the sea, in the Mariana Trench,
or divided among rose-colored rooms of mushroom houses,
or the mirrored caverns of a fernery. It could
be there. Might the states of the union, rather,
be wrapped across the face of a grass-covered ball?
If on an artichoke, plum-purple, will it tumble
in the sea? Or a grass-covered head?
If on the head with the boulder-strewn forests,
then the mountain is a man-like landform.
It is a place where statues are used as habitations.
And the people live in the head of one gigantic
statue—a colossus. And the rural landscape,
the hills, the windmills and the yellowing pastures,
come together to form the features of a man:
and the man's cat is a calico cat,
its whiskers as long as pine needles—indeed
they are pine needles. The cat, called Evergreen,
is curled up beside the rowboats:
it wakes up and stretches, digging its claws into larkspur.
It is handled gently by a girl
who puts her book down,
open with its pages lying flat on the table, daydreams,
as the "distant eccentric perturbers" (as the astronomers
have taken to calling the planets) shine above her.

The marjoram leans down to touch her, or the ferns
nod down toward her then quickly spring away.
Not far away, warm loaves of bread are taken
straight from the ovens and placed in baskets,
brought to the valley, and set beside
bottles of golden wine.

9 What?

An immense statue of a 9.
An immense 9 made of eleven
different minerals, shining,
bristling with the tricolor
flags of seven nations.
Are there nine things? Is this
figure of onyx and basalt
saying there is something 9
or that there are nine things
arranged somewhere for your awe,
your contemplation, your
delectation? Does this immortalize
nine things among quintillions
of all others? Would you like
nine or are you 9 as nine leaves
or beaded grapes? There is
a curve, a bend in the materials,
a sickle; there is sea kelp
plucked by the far trim sextant.
It is standing tall, black
in the green rain, a billboard.
When the sun comes out kids play

in its 9-shaped shadow.
Look—it has long since ceased
being an eyesore: it just slumps
now, the wet and wilted flags
like lettuce in a dead sandwich.
Who will intervene as it molders away
and nature does its work, decodes
what it was first meant to say
when a crane erected it with
scaffolding and pulleys. Oh,
what a cold thought it is to think,
that chill numeral, perhaps
a "useful idiot," perhaps the stone
paragon of an amoral universe.
In its inner curve a bird has built
its nest of twigs and roots and moss
as if in memory of poor John Clare,
who sleeps in a parallel world
in the top half of number 8.

Study of Blue

Think of a poem, concise—
concise to the point of obscurity.
And it is very clear, with
the clarity of a simple thing
seen through blue lenses:
a blue chair in a nearly empty
room, a table with a tea set
laid out for glass dolls: nothing
stirs; a potted fern, its thin
fronds brushing the ceiling,
and a fan-like piece
of pink and desiccated coral
in a glass frame. Is it obscure?
There is no obfuscation, where
light is the obliterant, milk-blue,
shadowing the obverse side
of edible ferns. It is
oblivious to what is asked of it,
tall and nearly so blue that it
is a slab of pure obsidian,
made of pure and simple atoms—
blue atoms; it is perfect
objectivity.

When I Was in Your Presence

When I was in your presence, like a cat,
your lucky star was in the sky.
A cat just stretches out and sleeps,
half its body in the sun.
We are all living here in a world-class city,
awake or asleep, full of flowering plants
and people on the move, all holding to dear brilliance,
a fairyland where danger is sublime, and vice versa.
A ray appears and dazzles the eye. The taffrail
is glittering in starlight, our ship
is stern, and you are watching the ignition
of incendiary events above the leaf-like buildings
on the starboard side; blinding treasures
furnishing all that surrounds your inner life
with an adorning lightness.

Noh

Remember the Noh plays of Japan?
The simple struggles of mortals,
the people turned to deer or stars or rain
in the molten forest, like pear-shaped pieces
of glass that burst into fragments when touched
by a human hand or the rain or the human-like hand
of the reaching catalpa. When we were newcomers
and Meistersingers in the oval and the round Megatherium,
we learned the quick lessons, as if bred for a thousand
years to be tame and wild by turns, like striped
cats sleeping, flying children patterned after wild ghosts
of children passing through. I wanted my son
to be as beautiful as the skyscrapers of the city,
beautiful and august, private and hard-going,
Mélisande of spirits, brain a half-opened book
where the glacier, virginal and bright,
is reminding us again that we are transformed children.

The Curiously Parallel

Inclination of a Girl's Head

A friend of mine has a great bush of sage
at the top of a gray wall, where the gray leaves
look shy and aloof. Sage is ornamental
as well as virtuous. You must make something of it,
and the fragile shadow of the sweet geranium,
the other melancholy, night-scented flowers.
There's a boll weevil on one—on another
a small snake . . . a garden snake or a bug, a bug
with the head of a snake.
And there's a primrose with the small head
of a girl—an angry girl, by the looks of her.
Her stepmother planted her there, near the rock
crystal, near the pond with the mallows
and the big stone head of a bearded man
half-submerged in the middle. It appears
that she committed some minor infraction,
like mistake a china doll's head for a turnip.
And as she blooms, just before she's snipped off
by a scissor, a celestial music purls forth
from a cloud, and a slice of bread and butter
comes drifting down on a yellow saucer.

The Sea and Its Children

Stick to the decorum, bright
as it is—and if you know
what it is, all the better.
Otherwise, you might rely
on what is written, for example,
on a handwritten pamphlet
taped to the window of a deli,
or the far-fetched explanations
of children. And if one tells you
she has a foot-long beetle kept
in gentle captivity, you might
be refreshed by its purple iridescence,
or help her release it into
the wild grass of the scrapyard,
and tell her that a package full of doll clothes
will arrive from Hong Kong
in the morning. On the spectrum
of the earth's inanimate objects,
the ocean is surely the closest
to the art of arranging flowers,
where silk-covered wire is used
to make toy dragonflies;
and it is the biggest, too,

the most maternal, the one
that bestows a consciousness
on sunset. It has a child
named Earth, and another called
Death, and like all mothers
it favors neither one
nor the other, as it sings both
to sleep in a humdrum town
with smog and acid rain.

Refinery in a Winter Landscape

There is some kind of refinery smoking
on the horizon—what kind is it?
And what might it be refining?
Is it distilling? Crushing
or processing? I don't know—perhaps
you can ask the experts? Holy Smokestacks!
Are there experts? Still to be seen. Could it be
one of the Little Fables about the earth?
Or around the earth? One of the figural shapes
like the knotted spandrels of an Asia
Minor rug, where the dragon is a symbol
for the infinite; the stork, long life; the duck
felicity; the bat, happiness; the butterfly,
the spirit? Bird is flight; peacock is paradise;
and then there is Idea, for which there is no
creature, laid down across the background
of the modern era. Here were the farmlands
of Pennsylvania. And that refinery,
that structure, alone, austere—
just standing there, serious
as a bird-headed man, a man with bird eyes,
with bird's wings folded up awaiting bird thoughts

to make some decision in front of the saffron-yellow sky.
He is also, as you'd guess, vertical,
and he has heavy-metal hair, magnetic,
a cigar inflated with leaves and infused with beryl . . .
and he is eating an eggplant.

The Orphan Girl in the
Wood Named Ericka Scissors

When the orphan girl lived
with her adopted grandfather in the woods,
the great woods of the black forest,
she collected her salad from among
the green things in the woods;
and when the wood was in its black mood,
or its green mood, still the light
on the golden foxtails glittered;
and she gathered marbled wood.
It was a lacquered group of leaves
for the paraffin salad. And when
she turned fifteen, the magical number
for all girls in haunted woods and orphan woods,
she longed to be taken from the forest,
and its junk of a million shades of green,
the wood painted with its one idea,
a green shambles of green bric-a-brac, it seemed.
And every day she sang the song that all girls
sing when they wake up trapped
in their very own lives:

Take me anywhere but here—
O tireless Rocketeer—
O Recorder—
Take me anywhere but here—

The Sea That Has Become Known

And as all things go off beyond the gaslight
to settle on the so-called bottom
of the so-called subconsciousness serenely,
at rest but lifting their bulk
above the waters and into the light
from time to time, we have repaired
to the upper room of the lighthouse,
the cool corner where we'd live
far above our past lives that stand out
brightly in the moments
when the strobes flicker over them,
because, as we have learned
through hard teaching, the sea
was a wild and obtuse mother.

And while we were brewing Sleep Tea
with the leaves of immense vegetation,
we turned the pages of Johannes Kepler's *Somnium*
where it is written, among the animadversions
for hope and perseverance, instructions
for all that has been forgotten
among the lunar features

in the wave of the sea called the Sea
That Has Become Known, or the sea called
the Sea of Islands, in the chains of craters
once called Summer, others called Lucretius;
lakes called Lake of Autumn, of Hatred,
of Death, of the Sea of the Blossoming of April,
where time will not obtain.

Family Seated around a Table

Family seated at the table at the end of day:
a mother and father, presumably; and a girl of twelve.
The teacup and the kettle are cream with a green glaze.
The knife is silver. The utensils are apricot, and red,
and shaped like fish. And there they were:
small family seated around a table at the end of day.
For one of them, the nearly transparent teacup close at hand.
For another, the small book called *Mustard Seed Garden*.
And for the third an air of remoteness.

(Open the door to the next room a bit wider.
A houseplant with five fan-like leaves
on a glass-topped table in a bright room—
and a painting on the wall: a low horizon
of pale yellow hills, and a giant cloud
billowing up from behind them.)

At the end of day, the three people seated
at the table stayed very still. And on the table
between them: one egg the color of hyacinth,
roseate and glowing gently . . .

The City That Would Never Be Finished

The Library of Alexandria: was it real?
Who can say? They say it held every book ever written.
It was *the* library of the ancient world. It held
the lost plays of Sophocles, pandects on astronomy
and architecture, studies on minerals on long
lapis lazuli–tinted sheets. It had comprehensive
lists of walls and bridges, epic poems, a giant pomona
illustrated with all the apples of the Hesperides
and a study on the pomegranate; there were hexaglot
theogonies, theophanies, scripts for puppet theaters,
accounts of harrowing battles and maritime disasters;
and your favorite book when young: *The Golden Book
of the Mysterious*. Look into the sky—then back again:
your biography and all things appertaining
were there too, where we were living congruent lives, coinciding
when superimposed, even over distance, over
time, the specters just rose petals in the solstice,
all sunset fires mirroring stone artifacts, cities
honeycombed in radiances flashing on the armories
and stairways built into the cliffside dwellings.
And I watched you there, dreaming away at your books
in the Rose Reading Room, the ceiling decorated

with golden clouds and plaster foliage winding
its sprays of wild florescence through trophies
emblematic of the seasons, fantastic birds
and bunches of grapes. And then I left
and walked down Fifth Avenue in a long coat
under banners waving from the mullions:
it was the fifth avenue of a city that would never be finished.

An 18th-Century Sunset

with Samuel Delany

From Halldór Laxness's *Under the Glacier*
we learned about glass in the heyday of cutting.
Yet it seems I robbed my gray-eyed child
of yet another experience: reading the *Kalevala*
in a tent during the polar vortex,
at the edge of the city where you can lease
one thousand palaces for free, and where Samuel
Delany is sitting in a café, his beard
growing across the table and down to the floor,
moss on his statuesque face, chirping
things in the plackets of his shirtsleeves.
He wrote a book about Thomas Alva Edison
that lights up once every hundred years,
each comet year, like the thunderbird
that rises from an herb bed of its own ashes
and shines. Foxes are covering the mountains.
Mushrooms are growing on the foxes.
People in the town are looking at the sunset.
It is a mere sunset—an 18th-century sunset.
Then it is a 19th-century sunset. Then

at last it's a 16th-century sunset,
styled so, of bitter-green opal
into which he walked one thousand miles
in one thousand successive hours in a silk hat
and a velveteen cravat on a drunken wager.
There is only the appearance of calm
as he pauses, stands there, still and proud:
a tiger petrified inside a grape.

A Voice Recording

Somebody probably touched a glass pane
beyond which a discordant sound
seemed to make its appeal
to your attention. You might
recognize one hundred men through
the most inventive disguises
but then pass by the friend
you have known since childhood,
smoking a cigar on the weather-beaten
deck of an old ship. Now
both he and you are in your manhood
and sleep where they grow green mushrooms
in rose rooms. But you're still
strangers. Smooth stones full of light
line the path and point the way
from the harbor to the meadow
where a big thawing out seems
to have taken place. I seem
to have entered a sphere of invisibility
where all things can take place near me
yet apart, tall and aloof as the eleven-shaped
clock. Then I step out of the sphere

and the tall grass bends, a jackrabbit
speckled with brown and flecked
with black and gold looks through me,
then into my eyes, then runs away.

What Happens to the World
When You Close a Book?

We have to doubt everything we feel.
And so, we are here, in the 21st century,
writing poems. We have to suspect parody—
yet the earth is a cool ceramic ball,
and we revolve, pellucid, in the sun,
while the icy cucumber and the warm‑blooded
eggplant ripen. And we must also
be carpenters from birth, for we are
living in the homes that we constructed:
circular walls or walls with circular breezeways
at the end of which rises a view of the sea—
and you can be equally divided between
those places, or several more.
And there are blocks of houses shut off
from one another by a wall of ferns.
But you can walk through rooms
you might have been in once,
and they're shut off from one another, too.
We were taught to fear nothing,
but a protective shell made of crystal

builds around you a fragile reticence,
and as siege machinery to centipede
is metaphor for mind or its strange
vacancy, its harmony ensues, is calmed—
interlocking hallways wind through
the interiors of buildings, and you
are reclining in sunbeams.

Reading Gibbon

Did you know that somewhere in a town
called Little Mexico a man reclines
in the green-shaded Burmese lamplight
reading Gibbon's *Decline and Fall of the Roman
Empire*? And that in Year 1, there were
already thousands of cities and towns,
and arched and towering aqueducts carried
water down from the encircling mountains
and into the public waterworks, the fountains
in the urban parks, and the vast hydraulic
system that kept the mill wheels turning
and the cisterns brimming with ice-cold
apples and ice-cold quenching water?
And that a man might wake up
and check the late hour
on the exhibition clock nailed to the seawall,
then turn and find a golden kit beside him?
He is sober, alert, and a cigarillo
smolders in the glass ashtray beside his head.

Glass in the Heyday of Cutting

It was is if we were moving
toward the fragrant center of the rose
where it seemed we were subdued
under the meridian's auspice, or aegis;
and there was a bee there, too, who had come into the rose,
and she was ever more at ease there than you and I,
where the water, dew on the rose, was home,
and whose long red lights shone across and onto far-flung
places. (And I forgot to say rose petals were all around us—
as any child could tell you if she were in our place.)

The red planet ascended the night sky by degrees,
and red crabs scuttled toward the courthouse where
the rocks are piled haphazardly to glow.
And the hunters and runners of classic renown,
Orion and Actaeon among them, had been turned
to stars or creatures of the forest—as in the days
we ate cactus and mushrooms, and it was your birthday;
we knew the mother should have the honor, for it was, verily,
her Birth-Giving Day, and as she was still among us,
it appeared, or among us now if only for one more day
before a billion days of rest, watering aspidistras and thyme

in jars and earthenware pots—ask the question
of her that can only be answered now, for these
few seconds as the sunset makes the silken wine
for strangers wine for everyone. But if you don't,
and miss the moment, and years seem to flicker,
clairvoyant, in the spruces,
her ghost might still pause and turn to you—

Deneb in Zenith

There was a beautiful greenhouse
on one of the rings of Saturn.
And within this greenhouse were forests,
ferns in warm rain, the reaching purple
vetch and the wise banyan, all tended
by a man and three gentle
duck‑like robots with watering cans.
But it was time to blow them up.

Are you, like me, easily swayed
by what is suggested by these things,
and do you turn with a strangely cold volition
like the sunflower toward the sun,
but find something there other than the sun,
though broad and sun‑like and showering down
green rays, green as rainbows in whose light
you might look at this cantaloupe?
It has a taste. And it has a smell.
And it recalls a time of flowered valleys,
where things were growing all over
and over the Valleys of Peace.

But let's not exploit this idea further.
Nature tells us everything once,
and under the mahogany and under the Lyre,
and under Deneb in Zenith, you must
consecrate yourself in the agony
of labor, the trance
after radiant birth.

So we leave them there, in the silence
in which we found them, alive and calm
in sunbeams, far distant from
the petroleum refineries of Earth—
amid the unfolding nocturnal flowers
of a dark and endless summer.
But then again, you can also choose to do nothing
(like a tree or a plant in sunbeams), and mean nothing,
like these trees and plants, alive and calm,
that are crowding around you in a blur of green.

Giant Moth Perishes

Giant moth perishes: this was what
the exorcist listened to when staring
into space. And to think that even small praises,
very small, are wrought among vines on Syrian jars,
and upon the jars of Persia. And birds
are in the vines, among the praises,
calling down among the nightshades
where the giant moth perishes.
And she brushes the enormous infrastructure
with her wings.

The Gathering Sea

Proctors on break
Wade knee-deep
In the low Brazilian tide.

*

Icelandic novels
On the lounge chairs
By the swimming pool.

*

Ate the red-yellow
Sansa apple. Dreamed
Of sex with Luz.

Roots, bulbs,
Green fleshy succulents
Growing on the soles of my feet.

*

Black headscarf.
Breasts
Swollen with milk.

*

Orange wind socks.
Blue warehouses
Across the still estuary.

Water from melting snow
Drips down a stairwell
Into a nursery filled with rubble.

*

On the tall bridge pylons
Welders lower
Black visors.

*

Snowman, teeth clenched,
Glares angrily
Into the trees.

Turning the page
Of the hexaglot Bible
Like the covers of a great, dark bed.

*

Put the pinking shears
Beneath the aspidistras;
Then complete the tangram.

*

The evergreen
Sangfroid gears
In November wind

A pool of red spillage
Cools
Adjacent to the blast furnace.

*

In the dry cleaner's window—
Spindles of red and yellow thread
While the snow falls.

*

I got to be here in the tide,
And at your breast,
Autumn near.

Machinery sparkles
On the new-mown
Baseball diamond.

*

Cold cider flowing from the presses.
Blue newspapers
Flowing from the presses.

*

In the hidden backyard
The small rabbit statues
Are covered with moss.

Ruminants wandering
The field behind
The dilapidated firehouse.

*

A fox
Slips through the fence
Across the flower bulbs.

*

The red-gold tubers
Smolder
In their bitter precinct.

Leave your leaf-green umbrella
On the doorstep.
Darjeeling is brewing in the breakfast room.

*

In the narrow space
Between a cyclone fence and a retaining wall—
Weeds and milk crates.

*

In the weedy backyard
Of an old duplex,
A lecture by Idi Amin.

The Sabbath elevators
Running all night
In the new wing of the children's hospital.

*

It is junk.
It is green junk.
It's kept in stacks in the grass.

*

Behind the rectory:
Clean cement, a pathway, and a fence with blackberry vines.
Above the rectory: clouds.

Lepidopterist dozing in the woods:
A giant blue moth
Opens and closes its wings on your shoulder.

*

"I hate the 100 doll eyes
In the kids' room, honey."
"So back out slowly."

*

Ice-green limes
Grow wild
On hedges by the path lights.

Now, your lavender shirt
Is slick
With sea bream.

*

Ultramodern
Makeshift
Icicle cities.

*

A ship
Small and toy-like
Next to the tremendous ice shelf.

Spread over several dark acres
The power plant
For the cathedral.

*

These brightly colored toys
Were mass-produced
In Chinese factories.

*

Blanch the parable
In the alpine waters
Where the icy fruits are blueing.

Mrs. Fountain, meet
The archangelical
Landgrave of St. Albans.

*

This is the nerve center:
Observe
The wildly sleeping babies.

*

They're dismantling the old bridge
In sight
Of the sugar refinery.

A pink building
In a landscape
Of glistening black minerals.

*

One day,
When I was 48 hours old,
It was a spring day, raining.

*

The elevator doors open
Onto a busy kitchen
And a Chinese wedding.

Folded note from a stranger:
"Destroy an apple
With your mind."

*

Sail-like leaves of chard
Growing wild in the space
Between the substation and the iron gate.

*

The patterned spray
Of the municipal fountain
Blown sideways in a gale.

Envelope dropped
In forsythia, return address
A Chinese fishery.

*

The green flag
Of a defunct African republic
Drying on a clothesline.

*

A shard of milky pink glass,
Its edges dulled,
Washed up on the seagrass.

Dream game:
Keep the armatures
From touching the apples.

*

Using calipers
To measure spiders
On the woodbine.

*

A rusty fan blade
Spinning in the window
Of an abandoned warehouse.

Weather stripping on the sides
Of tumbledown houses—
Humans dwelling on the earth.

*

An immense satellite dish
Tilted upward
Beside the abandoned granary.

*

In the overgrown sculpture garden:
A headless rabbit
Made of solid nicotine.

Above the tree line
The great white dome of the observatory
Turning toward the stars.

*

Cucumbers,
Green and pentecostal
In the boxcar.

*

Giant sheet of steel
Reflecting sunlight
Into the valley town.

Exterminator
Carrying his can of toxins
Through the snow.

*

The thump of cars
Crossing the bridge
Past the Municipal Asphalt Plant.

*

In dream, my salad,
Spiky, kale-green,
Attacks me.

Under the sun:
A basket of nails;
An acre of sunflowers.

*

Calculate
The angle of repose
Of a mound of broken glass.

*

In the giant wild lettuce
Behind the playground,
Rats thrive quietly.

It's raining.
There's a mildewed statue of an owl
By potted plants on the stairway.

*

Hidden somewhere in the eclogue:
A rabbit
In giant yellow pepper leaves.

*

At sunset
A door
And the gathering sea.

Acknowledgments

Some of the poems in this book appeared in *Foundry*, *On the Seawall*, and *Washington Square Review*.

My love and gratitude to these friends who closely read this book in parts or in its entirety and gave valuable feedback: Tom King, Cort Day, David Joel Friedman, Anthony Madrid, Mark Levine, Molly Lou Freeman, Mark Faunlagui, and Regan Good.

And my deep gratitude to the people at Wave Books: my friend and editor Matthew Zapruder, Charlie Wright, Blyss Ervin, Heidi Broadhead, Catherine Bresner, and Joshua Beckman.

"Giant Moth Perishes" is the name of a composition by Brent Arnold. Thank you, Brent, for letting me borrow it.

A charge transmitted and gift occult for those being born. —Walt Whitman